♡mom
10-12

Contents

Christmastime Classics 2

Merry Brownies & Bars 22

Sugarplum Fun 40

Yuletide Treasures 60

Holiday Express 80

Acknowledgments 94

Index 95

Christmastime Classics

Candy-Studded Wreaths

1 cup (2 sticks) unsalted butter, softened
½ cup powdered sugar
2 tablespoons packed light brown sugar
1 teaspoon vanilla
¼ teaspoon salt
2 cups all-purpose flour
   Green food coloring
   Mini candy-coated chocolate pieces

1. Beat butter, powdered sugar, brown sugar, vanilla and salt in large bowl with electric mixer at medium speed 2 minutes or until light and fluffy. Gradually add flour, beating well after each addition.

2. Divide dough in half. Tint one half of dough with food coloring until desired shade of green is reached. (If dough is too soft to handle, wrap in plastic wrap and refrigerate about 1 hour.)

3. Preheat oven to 300°F. Shape green dough into 28 (5-inch) ropes. Repeat with plain dough. For each wreath, twist one green and one plain rope together; press ends together. Place on ungreased cookie sheets. Press 4 to 6 chocolate pieces into each wreath.

4. Bake 15 to 18 minutes or until cookies are set and lightly browned. Cool on cookie sheets 5 minutes; remove to wire racks to cool completely. *Makes 28 cookies*

Candy-Studded Wreaths

Extra-Chocolatey Brownie Cookies

2 cups all-purpose flour
½ cup unsweetened Dutch process cocoa powder
1 teaspoon baking soda
¾ teaspoon salt
1 cup (2 sticks) butter, softened
1 cup packed brown sugar
½ cup granulated sugar
2 eggs
2 teaspoon vanilla
1 package (11½ ounces) semisweet chocolate chunks or chips
2 cups coarsely chopped walnuts or pecans

1. Preheat oven to 375°F. Whisk flour, cocoa, baking soda and salt in medium bowl until well blended.

2. Beat butter in large bowl with electric mixer at medium speed 1 minute or until light and creamy. Add brown sugar and granulated sugar; beat 2 minutes or until fluffy. Add eggs and vanilla; beat until well blended. Add flour mixture; beat at low speed until blended. Stir in chocolate chunks and walnuts.

3. Drop dough by heaping tablespoonfuls about 2 inches apart onto ungreased cookie sheets. Flatten dough slightly with back of spoon.

4. Bake 12 minutes or until edges are browned. Cool on cookie sheets 2 minutes; remove to wire racks to cool completely. Store in airtight container at room temperature up to 4 days. *Makes 3 dozen cookies*

Prep Time: 20 minutes
Bake Time: 12 minutes

Extra-Chocolatey Brownie Cookies

Snowball Surprises

1 cup (2 sticks) butter, softened
¾ cup powdered sugar, divided
1 teaspoon vanilla
1¾ cups all-purpose flour
¼ teaspoon salt
1 cup pecan halves, toasted* and finely chopped
1 bar (3 ounces) chocolate candy with almonds, broken into
    36 (½-inch) pieces

To toast pecans, spread in single layer on cookie sheet. Bake in preheated 350°F oven 8 to 10 minutes or until golden brown, stirring frequently.

1. Lightly grease cookie sheets or line with parchment paper. Beat butter and ½ cup powdered sugar in large bowl until well blended. Add vanilla; beat until blended. Gradually add flour and salt, beating after each addition. Stir in pecans.

2. Shape dough by tablespoonfuls into 36 balls. Press chocolate piece into each dough ball, working dough around chocolate to cover. Place balls 1½ inches apart on prepared cookie sheets. Refrigerate 30 minutes to 1 hour or until dough is firm.

3. Preheat oven to 350°F. Bake cookies 13 to 15 minutes or until edges are lightly browned. Remove to wire racks to cool slightly. Sprinkle remaining ¼ cup powdered sugar over warm cookies.

Makes 3 dozen cookies

 **Quick Tip**

To soften butter quickly, place two sticks of butter
on a microwavable plate and heat on LOW (30%)
about 40 seconds or just until softened.

Snowball Surprises

Gingerbread People

½ cup (1 stick) butter, softened
½ cup packed brown sugar
⅓ cup water
⅓ cup molasses
1 egg
4 cups all-purpose flour
2 teaspoons baking soda
1 teaspoon ground ginger
½ teaspoon ground allspice
½ teaspoon ground cinnamon
½ teaspoon ground cloves
   Assorted icings and candies

1. Beat butter and brown sugar in large bowl with electric mixer at medium speed until creamy. Add water, molasses and egg; beat until blended. Add flour, baking soda, ginger, allspice, cinnamon and cloves; beat until well blended. Shape dough into disc; wrap tightly with plastic wrap. Refrigerate about 2 hours or until firm.

2. Preheat oven to 350°F. Grease cookie sheets. Roll out dough on lightly floured surface with lightly floured rolling pin to ⅛-inch thickness. Cut out dough with cookie cutter. Place cutouts 2 inches apart on prepared cookie sheets.

3. Bake 12 to 15 minutes or until set. Cool on cookie sheets 1 minute; remove to wire racks to cool completely. Decorate as desired. Store in airtight containers. *Makes about 4½ dozen cookies*

Gingerbread People

Cut-Out Cookies

3½ cups all-purpose flour
2 teaspoons baking powder
¼ teaspoon salt
1 (14-ounce) can EAGLE BRAND® Sweetened Condensed Milk
  (NOT evaporated milk)
¾ cup (1½ sticks) butter or margarine, softened
2 eggs
1 tablespoon vanilla extract
Colored sugar sprinkles (optional)
Powdered Sugar Glaze (optional, recipe follows)

1. In small bowl, combine flour, baking powder and salt; set aside.

2. In large bowl with mixer on low speed, beat EAGLE BRAND®, butter, eggs and vanilla until just combined. Beat on medium speed 1 minute until smooth. Add flour mixture; beat on low speed until combined. (If using hand-held mixer, use wooden spoon to add last portion of flour mixture.) Divide dough into thirds. Wrap and chill dough 2 hours or until easy to handle.

3. Preheat oven to 350°F. On lightly floured surface, roll out one portion of dough to ⅛-inch thickness. Cut out shapes with floured cookie cutters. Reroll as necessary to use all dough. Place cut-outs 1 inch apart on ungreased baking sheets. Sprinkle with colored sugar (optional).

4. Bake 9 to 11 minutes or until very lightly browned around edges (do not overbake). Cool. Glaze and decorate (optional). Remove cookies to wire racks. Store leftovers loosely covered at room temperature. Or, freeze in tightly sealed container. *Makes 5½ dozen cookies*

Powdered Sugar Glaze

2 cups sifted powdered sugar
½ teaspoon vanilla extract
2 tablespoons milk or whipping cream
Food coloring (optional)

Combine sugar and vanilla, adding just enough milk to make glaze consistency. Add food coloring (optional) to tint glaze.

Cut-Out Cookies

Chocolate Oatmeal Chippers

1¼ cups all-purpose flour
½ cup NESTLÉ® TOLL HOUSE® Baking Cocoa
1 teaspoon baking soda
¼ teaspoon salt
1 cup (2 sticks) butter or margarine, softened
1 cup packed brown sugar
½ cup granulated sugar
1 teaspoon vanilla extract
2 eggs
1¾ cups (11½-ounce package) NESTLÉ® TOLL HOUSE®
    Milk Chocolate Morsels
1¾ cups quick or old-fashioned oats
1 cup chopped nuts (optional)

PREHEAT oven to 375°F.

COMBINE flour, cocoa, baking soda and salt in medium bowl. Beat butter, brown sugar, granulated sugar and vanilla in large mixer bowl until creamy. Beat in eggs. Gradually beat in flour mixture. Stir in morsels, oats and nuts. Drop dough by rounded tablespoon onto ungreased baking sheets.

BAKE for 9 to 12 minutes or until edges are set but centers are still soft. Cool on baking sheets for 2 minutes; remove to wire racks to cool completely.   *Makes about 4 dozen cookies*

Bar Cookie Variation: **PREHEAT** oven to 350°F. Grease 15×10-inch jelly-roll pan. Prepare dough as above. Spread into prepared pan. Bake for 25 to 30 minutes. Cool in pan on wire rack. Makes about 4 dozen bars.

Chocolate Oatmeal Chippers

Apricot-Pecan Tassies

1 cup all-purpose flour
½ cup (1 stick) plus 1 tablespoon butter, cut into pieces, divided
6 tablespoons cream cheese
¾ cup packed light brown sugar
1 egg
½ teaspoon vanilla
¼ teaspoon salt
⅔ cup diced dried apricots
⅓ cup chopped pecans

1. Place flour, ½ cup butter and cream cheese in food processor; process with on/off pulses until mixture forms a ball. Wrap dough in plastic wrap; refrigerate 15 minutes.

2. Preheat oven to 325°F. Grease 24 mini (1¾-inch) muffin cups or line with paper baking cups.

3. Beat brown sugar, egg, remaining 1 tablespoon butter, vanilla and salt with electric mixer at medium speed until creamy. Stir in apricots and pecans.

4. Shape dough into 24 balls; place in prepared muffin cups. Press dough on bottom and up side of each cup. Fill each cup with 1 teaspoon apricot mixture. Bake 25 minutes or until light golden brown. Cool in pans on wire racks. *Makes 2 dozen cookies*

 Quick Tip

Try using kitchen scissors to cut up dried apricots—it can be quicker and easier than using a knife.

Apricot-Pecan Tassies

Holiday Sugar Cookies

1 cup (2 sticks) butter, softened
¾ cup sugar
1 egg
2 cups all-purpose flour
1 teaspoon baking powder
¼ teaspoon salt
¼ teaspoon ground cinnamon
   Colored sugar or sprinkles (optional)

1. Beat butter and sugar in large bowl with electric mixer at medium speed until creamy. Add egg; beat until fluffy.

2. Stir in flour, baking powder, salt and cinnamon until well blended. Shape dough into disc; wrap tightly with plastic wrap. Refrigerate about 2 hours or until firm.

3. Preheat oven to 350°F. Roll small portion of dough to ¼-inch thickness on lightly floured surface with lightly floured rolling pin. (Keep remaining dough wrapped in refrigerator.)

4. Cut out dough with 3-inch cookie cutters. Decorate with colored sugar or sprinkles; place on ungreased cookie sheets. Repeat with remaining dough.

5. Bake 7 to 9 minutes until edges are lightly browned. Cool on cookie sheets 1 minute; remove to wire racks to cool completely. Store in airtight container.   *Makes about 3 dozen cookies*

Holiday Sugar Cookies

Pistachio Cranberry Biscotti

Cookie
- 1 package (about 17 ounces) sugar cookie mix
- ⅓ cup butter, softened
- ¼ cup all-purpose flour
- 2 eggs, beaten
- 1 tablespoon grated orange peel
- ¾ cup pistachio nuts, chopped
- ½ cup dried cranberries or cherries

Icing
- 1 package (12 ounces) white chocolate chips
- 1 teaspoon shortening

1. Preheat oven 350°F. Line two large cookie sheets with parchment paper.

2. Combine cookie mix, butter, flour, eggs and orange peel in large bowl; stir until stiff dough forms. Stir in pistachios and cranberries. Divide dough into four pieces. Shape each piece into 10×1¼-inch log on lightly floured surface.

3. Place two logs on each baking sheet, leaving at least 3 inches between logs and sides of pans. Bake 20 to 22 minutes or until firm and golden brown. Cool on cookie sheets 10 minutes.

4. Remove logs to cutting board; cut diagonally into ½-inch slices with serrated knife. Place slices, cut side down, on cookie sheets. Bake 6 minutes; turn cookies and bake 6 minutes more. Remove to wire racks to cool completely.

5. Place white chocolate chips and shortening in medium microwavable bowl. Microwave on HIGH about 1½ minutes, stirring at 30-second intervals, until chocolate is melted and mixture is smooth. Dip one side of each biscotti into melted chocolate. Place on parchment or waxed paper to set. Store in airtight container. *Makes 4 dozen biscotti*

Pistachio Cranberry Biscotti

Holiday Treasure Cookies

1½ cups graham cracker crumbs
½ cup all-purpose flour
2 teaspoons baking powder
1 (14-ounce) can EAGLE BRAND® Sweetened Condensed Milk
   (NOT evaporated milk)
½ cup (1 stick) butter or margarine, softened
1⅓ cups flaked coconut
1¾ cups (10 ounces) mini kisses, milk chocolate or semisweet
   chocolate baking pieces
1 cup red and green holiday baking bits

1. Preheat oven to 375°F. In medium bowl, combine graham cracker crumbs, flour and baking powder; set aside.

2. Beat EAGLE BRAND® and butter until smooth; add reserved crumb mixture, mixing well. Stir in coconut, chocolate pieces and holiday baking bits. Drop by rounded teaspoonfuls onto greased cookie sheets.

3. Bake 7 to 9 minutes or until lightly browned. Cool 1 minute; transfer from cookie sheet to wire rack. Cool completely. Store leftovers tightly covered at room temperature.   *Makes about 5½ dozen cookies*

Chocolate Walnut Meringues

3 egg whites
   Pinch of salt
¾ cup sugar
½ cup good-quality Dutch-processed cocoa
⅓ cup finely chopped California walnuts

Preheat oven to 350°F. Beat egg whites and salt in large bowl with electric mixer or wire whisk until soft peaks form. Gradually add sugar, beating until stiff peaks form. Sift cocoa over peaks and fold into egg white mixture with walnuts. Spoon mounds about 1 inch in diameter and about 1 inch apart onto parchment-lined baking sheets. Bake 20 minutes or until dry to the touch. Cool completely before removing from baking sheets. Store in airtight container.   *Makes 48 cookies*

*Favorite recipe from **Walnut Marketing Board***

Holiday Treasure Cookies

Merry
Brownies & Bars

Butterscotch Toffee Gingersnap Squares

     40 gingersnap cookies
    ⅓ cup butter, melted
     1 can (14 ounces) sweetened condensed milk
    1½ teaspoons vanilla
     1 cup butterscotch chips
    ½ cup pecan pieces
    ½ cup chopped peanuts
    ½ cup toffee bits
    ½ cup mini semisweet chocolate chips

1. Preheat oven to 350°F. Line 13×9-inch baking pan with foil, leaving 1-inch overhang. Spray foil with nonstick cooking spray.

2. Place cookies in food processor; process until crumbs form. Measure out 2 cups.

3. Combine 2 cups crumbs and butter in medium bowl; mix well. Press crumb mixture evenly into bottom of prepared pan. Bake 4 to 5 minutes or until light brown around edges.

4. Meanwhile, combine condensed milk and vanilla in small bowl; pour over warm crust. Sprinkle with butterscotch chips, pecans, peanuts, toffee bits and chocolate chips. Press down gently.

5. Bake 15 to 18 minutes or until bubbly and golden. Cool completely in pan on wire rack. Remove foil; cut into bars. Store in airtight container. *Makes 3 dozen bars*

Butterscotch Toffee Gingersnap Squares

Perfectly Peppermint Brownies

¾ cup HERSHEY'S Cocoa
½ teaspoon baking soda
⅔ cup butter or margarine, melted and divided
½ cup boiling water
2 cups sugar
2 eggs
1⅓ cups all-purpose flour
1 teaspoon vanilla extract
¼ teaspoon salt
1⅓ cups (8-ounce package) YORK® Mini Peppermint Patties*

*16 to 17 small (1½-inch) YORK Peppermint Patties, unwrapped and coarsely chopped, may be substituted for the mini peppermint patties.

1. Heat oven to 350°F. Grease 13×9×2-inch baking pan.

2. Stir together cocoa and baking soda in large bowl; stir in ⅓ cup butter. Add boiling water; stir until mixture thickens. Stir in sugar, eggs and remaining ⅓ cup butter; stir until smooth. Add flour, vanilla and salt; blend completely. Stir in peppermint patties. Spread in prepared pan.

3. Bake 35 to 40 minutes or until brownies begin to pull away from sides of pan. Cool completely in pan on wire rack. Cut into bars.

Makes 36 brownies

Perfectly Peppermint Brownies

Cran-Orange Oatmeal Bars

½ cup (1 stick) butter, softened
½ cup dried cranberries
1 egg
1 teaspoon grated orange peel, divided
3 tablespoons orange juice, divided
1 package (about 17 ounces) oatmeal cookie mix
1 cup powdered sugar

1. Preheat oven to 375°F. Spray 13×9-baking dish with nonstick cooking spray.

2. Combine butter, cranberries, egg, ½ teaspoon orange peel and 1 tablespoon orange juice in medium bowl. Stir in cookie mix until well blended. Spread batter evenly in prepared baking dish.

3. Bake 17 minutes or until light golden brown around edges. Cool completely in pan on wire rack.

4. Blend powdered sugar and remaining 2 tablespoons orange juice in small bowl until smooth. Stir in remaining ½ teaspoon orange peel. Drizzle evenly over bars.   *Makes 2 dozen bars*

 **Quick Tip**

One medium orange will yield about ⅓ cup juice and
1 to 2 tablespoons grated peel.

Cran-Orange Oatmeal Bars

Ornament Brownies

6 squares (1 ounce each) semisweet chocolate, coarsely
    chopped
1 tablespoon instant coffee granules
1 tablespoon boiling water
¾ cup all-purpose flour
¾ teaspoon ground cinnamon
½ teaspoon baking powder
¼ teaspoon salt
½ cup sugar
¼ cup (½ stick) butter, softened
2 eggs
    Prepared white frosting
    Assorted food coloring
    Small candy canes
    Assorted candies and sprinkles

1. Preheat oven to 350°F. Grease 8-inch square baking pan. Place chocolate in small microwavable bowl. Microwave on HIGH 30 seconds; stir. Repeat as necessary until chocolate is melted. Dissolve coffee granules in boiling water; set aside.

2. Combine flour, cinnamon, baking powder and salt in small bowl. Beat sugar and butter in large bowl with electric mixer at medium speed until light and fluffy. Beat in eggs, 1 at a time. Beat in melted chocolate and coffee until well blended. Add flour mixture; beat at low speed until well blended. Spread batter evenly in prepared pan.

3. Bake 30 to 35 minutes or until center is set. Cool completely in pan on wire rack. Cut into holiday shapes using 2-inch cookie cutters.

4. Tint frosting with food coloring to desired colors. Spread over each brownie. Break off top of small candy cane to create loop; insert in top of brownie. Decorate as desired with assorted candies and sprinkles.

Makes about 8 brownies

Ornament Brownies

Pumpkin Cheesecake Squares

1½ cups gingersnap crumbs, plus additional for garnish
6 tablespoons butter, melted
2 eggs
¼ cup plus 2 tablespoons sugar, divided
2½ teaspoons vanilla, divided
1 package (8 ounces) plus 1 package (3 ounces) cream cheese, softened
1¼ cups solid-pack pumpkin
1 teaspoon ground cinnamon
¼ teaspoon ground ginger
¼ teaspoon ground nutmeg
¼ teaspoon ground cloves
1 cup sour cream

1. Preheat oven to 325°F. Lightly grease 13×9-inch baking pan.

2. Combine 1½ cups crumbs and butter in small bowl. Press into bottom of prepared pan. Bake 10 minutes.

3. Meanwhile, combine eggs, ¼ cup sugar and 1½ teaspoons vanilla in food processor or blender. Process 1 minute or until smooth. Add cream cheese and pumpkin; process until well blended. Stir in cinnamon, ginger, nutmeg and cloves. Pour mixture evenly over hot crust. Bake 40 minutes.

4. For topping, whisk sour cream, remaining 2 tablespoons sugar and 1 teaspoon vanilla in small bowl until blended. Remove cheesecake from oven; spread sour cream mixture evenly over top. Bake 5 minutes. Turn off oven; open door halfway and let cheesecake cool in oven. When cool, refrigerate 2 hours. Sprinkle with additional gingersnap crumbs; cut into squares.   *Makes about 3 dozen squares*

Pumpkin Cheesecake Squares

Cranberry Coconut Bars

Filling

    2 cups fresh or frozen cranberries
    1 cup dried sweetened cranberries
    $\frac{2}{3}$ cup granulated sugar
    $\frac{1}{4}$ cup water
    Grated peel of 1 lemon

Crust

    1$\frac{1}{4}$ cups all-purpose flour
    $\frac{3}{4}$ cup uncooked old-fashioned oats
    $\frac{1}{2}$ teaspoon baking soda
    $\frac{1}{2}$ teaspoon salt
    $\frac{3}{4}$ cup (1$\frac{1}{2}$ sticks) unsalted butter, softened
    1 cup packed light brown sugar
    1 cup shredded sweetened coconut
    1 cup chopped pecans, toasted*

To toast pecans, spread in single layer on baking sheet. Bake in preheated 350°F oven 5 to 7 minutes or until golden brown, stirring frequently.

1. Preheat oven to 400°F. Grease and flour 13×9-inch baking pan.

2. For filling, combine fresh cranberries, dried cranberries, granulated sugar, water and lemon peel in medium saucepan. Cook 10 to 15 minutes over medium-high heat until mixture is pulpy, stirring frequently. Mash cranberries with back of spoon. Cool to lukewarm.

3. For crust, combine flour, oats, baking soda and salt in medium bowl. Beat butter and brown sugar in large bowl with electric mixer at medium speed until creamy. Add flour mixture; beat just until blended. Stir in coconut and pecans. Reserve 1$\frac{1}{2}$ cups; press remaining crumb mixture into bottom of prepared pan. Bake 10 minutes.

4. Gently spread cranberry filling over crust. Sprinkle with reserved crumb mixture. Bake 18 to 20 minutes or until set and crust is golden brown. Cool completely in pan on wire rack. *Makes 2 dozen bars*

Note: You can make these bars when fresh or frozen cranberries aren't available. Prepare the filling using 2 cups dried sweetened cranberries, 1 cup water and the peel of 1 lemon; cook 8 to 10 minutes over medium heat, stirring frequently. Use as directed in step 4.

Cranberry Coconut Bars

"Mexican" Brownies

1 package (about 19 ounces) brownie mix, plus ingredients
    to prepare mix
2 teaspoons ground cinnamon
1 package (8 ounces) cream cheese, softened
½ cup dulce de leche (see Note)
2 tablespoons powdered sugar

1. Prepare and bake brownies according to package directions, stirring cinnamon into batter. Cool completely in pan on wire rack.

2. Beat cream cheese in medium bowl with electric mixer at medium speed until smooth. Add dulce de leche and sugar; beat until well blended and creamy.

3. Spread frosting over brownies. Serve immediately or refrigerate overnight for richer flavor. *Makes 16 brownies*

Note: Dulce de leche is caramelized condensed milk widely used in Mexican desserts. It is sold in cans in most large supermarkets. You can prepare your our own dulce de leche by heating 1 cup whole milk and ½ cup granulated sugar just to a boil; reduce the heat to medium-low and cook 30 minutes or until caramel in color, stirring occasionally. Remove from the heat and cool completely. Stir in ¼ teaspoon vanilla. If you are using homemade dulce de leche in this recipe, omit the powdered sugar.

"Mexican" Brownies

Chewy Pecan-Gingersnap Triangles

20 gingersnap cookies, broken in half
½ cup (1 stick) butter, softened
¼ cup granulated sugar
¼ cup packed light brown sugar
1 egg, separated
½ teaspoon vanilla
⅛ teaspoon salt
1 teaspoon water
1½ cups chopped pecan pieces (6 ounces)

1. Preheat oven to 350°F. Line bottom and sides of 13×9-inch baking pan with foil, leaving 2-inch overhang. Spray foil with nonstick cooking spray.

2. Place gingersnap cookies in food processor; process until crumbs form. (Or, cookies may be placed in resealable food storage bag and crushed with rolling pin or meat mallet.)

3. Beat butter, granulated sugar, brown sugar, egg yolk and vanilla in medium bowl with electric mixer until well blended. Add cookie crumbs and salt; mix well. Lightly press crumb mixture into bottom of prepared pan to form thin crust.

4. Whisk egg white and water in small bowl. Brush egg white mixture evenly over crust; sprinkle evenly with pecans. Press pecans in lightly to adhere to crust.

5. Bake 20 minutes or until lightly browned. Cool completely in pan on wire rack. Use foil handles to remove bars from pan to cutting board. Cut into 3-inch squares; cut squares diagonally in half.

Makes 2 dozen triangles

Chewy Pecan-Gingersnap Triangles

Fruitcake Bars

1 cup diced dried apricots
1 cup diced dates
2 tablespoons rum or orange juice
1 cup packed dark brown sugar
½ cup (1 stick) butter, softened
3 eggs
　Grated peel of 1 orange
1 teaspoon vanilla
1 cup all-purpose flour
¼ teaspoon salt
1½ cups chopped pecans, toasted*
1 cup semisweet chocolate chips
¾ cup white chocolate chips

To toast pecans, spread in single layer on baking sheet. Bake in preheated 350°F oven 8 to 10 minutes or until golden brown, stirring frequently.

1. Combine apricots, dates and rum in small bowl; let stand 30 minutes, stirring occasionally.

2. Preheat oven to 325°F. Grease 13×9-inch baking pan.

3. Beat brown sugar and butter in large bowl with electric mixer at medium speed until well blended. Add eggs, 1 at a time, beating well after each addition. Add orange peel and vanilla; beat until blended. Add flour and salt; beat until blended. Stir in dried fruit, pecans and semisweet chocolate chips. Spread batter in prepared pan.

4. Bake 35 minutes or until toothpick inserted into center comes out clean and edges begin to pull away from sides of pan.

5. Sprinkle with white chocolate chips; let stand until chips are spreadable. Spread chips gently over top of bars. Cool completely in pan on wire rack.　　　　*Makes about 2½ dozen bars*

Fruitcake Bars

Sugarplum
Fun

Crunchy Christmas Wreaths

22 red licorice strings (about 10 inches long)
½ cup (1 stick) butter
3 cups mini marshmallows
1 teaspoon vanilla
¼ teaspoon salt
   Green food coloring
5 to 5½ cups puffed corn cereal
⅓ cup mini candy-coated chocolate pieces (optional)

1. Line cookie sheets with waxed paper. Tie each licorice string into bow; set aside.

2. Melt butter in large heavy saucepan over low heat. Add marshmallows; stir until melted and smooth. Stir in vanilla and salt. Tint with food coloring until desired shade of green is reached. Add 5 cups cereal; stir until evenly coated. Add remaining ½ cup cereal, if necessary. Remove from heat.

3. Drop mixture by ¼ cupfuls onto prepared cookie sheets. With lightly greased hands, quickly shape each mound into 3-inch ring. Press licorice bow and candies onto each wreath as desired. Refrigerate 1 hour or until set. Store covered in refrigerator.

Makes 22 wreaths

Crunchy Christmas Wreaths

Holiday Buttons

2 cups all-purpose flour
¼ teaspoon salt
⅛ teaspoon baking powder
½ cup (1 stick) butter, softened
1¼ cups chocolate hazelnut spread, divided
⅓ cup granulated sugar
⅓ cup packed light brown sugar
1 egg
½ teaspoon almond extract
Decors, nonpareils or decorating sugar

1. Combine flour, salt and baking powder in small bowl. Beat butter, ½ cup chocolate-hazelnut spread, granulated sugar and brown sugar in large bowl with electric mixer at medium speed until well blended. Add egg and almond extract; beat until well blended. Gradually add flour mixture, beating after each addition.

2. Divide dough into 4 pieces; shape each piece into 7-inch log. Wrap in plastic wrap; refrigerate 2 to 3 hours or until firm.

3. Preheat oven to 325°F. Lightly grease cookie sheets or line with parchment paper. Cut dough into ⅜-inch-thick slices; place 1 inch apart on prepared cookie sheets. Poke 4 holes in slices with toothpick or straw.

4. Bake 12 to 14 minutes or until cookies are set. Cool on cookie sheets 1 minute; remove to wire racks to cool completely.

5. Spread 1 teaspoon chocolate-hazelnut spread on flat sides of half of cookies; top with remaining cookies. Roll sides of sandwich cookies in decors. *Makes 3½ dozen sandwich cookies*

Holiday Buttons

Malted Milk Cookies

1 cup (2 sticks) butter, softened
¾ cup granulated sugar
¾ cup packed light brown sugar
1 teaspoon baking soda
2 eggs
2 squares (1 ounce each) unsweetened chocolate, melted and
    cooled to room temperature
1 teaspoon vanilla
2¼ cups all-purpose flour
½ cup malted milk powder
1 cup chopped malted milk balls

1. Preheat oven to 375°F.

2. Beat butter in large bowl with electric mixer at medium speed until creamy. Add granulated sugar, brown sugar and baking soda; beat until blended. Add eggs, chocolate and vanilla; beat until well blended. Beat in flour and malted milk powder until blended. Stir in malted milk balls. Drop dough by rounded tablespoonfuls 2½ inches apart onto ungreased cookie sheets.

3. Bake about 10 minutes or until edges are firm. Cool on cookie sheets 1 minute; remove to wire racks to cool completely.

Makes about 3 dozen cookies

Quick Tip

Malted milk balls can be difficult to chop with a knife. If you don't mind more uneven pieces, place the malted milk balls in a resealable food storage bag, seal the bag and crush the candy with a meat mallet or rolling pin.

Malted Milk Cookies

Santa's Cookie Pizza

1½ cups all-purpose flour
¼ cup unsweetened cocoa powder
¼ teaspoon salt
¾ cup (1½ sticks) butter, slightly softened
¾ cup sugar
3 egg yolks
1 teaspoon vanilla
1 package (12 ounces) white chocolate chips
½ cup plus 1 tablespoon sweetened condensed milk, divided
1 cup mini pretzel twists
1 cup red and green gum drops
½ cup chopped peanuts
½ cup red and green chocolate candies

1. Preheat oven to 350°F. Lightly spray 12-inch round pizza pan with nonstick cooking spray.

2. Sift flour, cocoa and salt into small bowl. Beat butter and sugar in large bowl with electric mixer at medium speed 1 minute. Beat in egg yolks and vanilla until well blended. Add flour mixture; beat just until combined.

3. Press dough into pan, building up edges slightly. Refrigerate at least 15 minutes. Prick holes all over dough with fork. Bake 18 to 20 minutes or until firm. Remove to wire rack to cool slightly.

4. Heat white chocolate chips and ½ cup condensed milk in medium saucepan over low heat until chocolate is melted, stirring constantly. Reserve one fourth of chocolate mixture; spread remaining mixture evenly over crust. Immediately sprinkle with pretzels, gum drops, peanuts and candies, presssing down gently to adhere.

5. Combine remaining 1 tablespoon condensed milk and reserved chocolate mixture; stir over low heat until blended. Drizzle over pizza. Cool completely on wire rack before cutting into wedges. Store in airtight container. *Makes 16 wedges*

Santa's Cookie Pizza

PB & J Thumbprint Cookies

  2 cups uncooked old-fashioned oats
1⅓ cups plus 1 tablespoon all-purpose flour
  ¾ teaspoon baking soda
  ½ teaspoon baking powder
  ½ teaspoon salt
  1 cup packed brown sugar
  ¾ cup (1½ sticks) butter, softened
  ¼ cup granulated sugar
  ¼ cup chunky peanut butter
  1 egg
  1 tablespoon honey
  1 teaspoon vanilla
  ½ cup chopped peanuts, unsalted or honey-roasted
  ½ cup grape jelly or flavor of choice

1. Preheat oven to 350°F. Line cookie sheets with parchment paper.

2. Combine oats, flour, baking soda, baking powder and salt in medium bowl. Beat brown sugar, butter and granulated sugar in large bowl with electric mixer at medium speed until well blended. Beat at high speed until light and fluffy. Add peanut butter, egg, honey and vanilla; beat at medium speed until well blended. Gradually add flour mixture; beat just until blended. Stir in peanuts. Drop dough by rounded tablespoonfuls onto prepared cookie sheets.

3. Bake 10 minutes. Remove cookies from oven. Press center of each cookie with back of teaspoon to make a slight indentation; fill with about ½ teaspoon jelly. Return to oven; bake 4 to 6 minutes or until puffed and golden. Cool on cookie sheets 5 minutes; remove to wire racks to cool completely. *Makes about 40 cookies*

PB & J Thumbprint Cookies

Chocolate Gingerbread Cookies

2¼ cups all-purpose flour
3 tablespoons unsweetened cocoa powder
2½ teaspoons ground ginger
½ teaspoon baking soda
½ teaspoon ground cinnamon
⅛ teaspoon salt
⅛ teaspoon finely ground black pepper
½ cup (1 stick) unsalted butter, softened
½ cup packed light brown sugar
¼ cup granulated sugar
1 tablespoon shortening
4 squares (1 ounce each) semisweet chocolate, melted and cooled
2 tablespoons molasses
1 egg
Prepared icing (optional)

1. Combine flour, cocoa, ginger, baking soda, cinnamon, salt and pepper in medium bowl. Beat butter, brown sugar, granulated sugar and shortening in large bowl with electric mixer at medium speed until creamy. Add chocolate; beat until blended. Add molasses and egg; beat until well blended. Gradually add flour mixture, beating until well blended. Divide dough in half; form each half into disc. Wrap each disc tightly with plastic wrap; refrigerate at least 1 hour.

2. Preheat oven to 350°F. Roll out 1 disc dough between sheets of plastic wrap to ¼-inch thickness. Cut out dough with 5-inch cookie cutters; place cutouts on ungreased cookie sheets. Refrigerate at least 15 minutes. Repeat with remaining disc dough.

3. Bake 8 to 10 minutes or until cookies have puffed slightly and have small cracks. Cool on cookie sheets 5 minutes; remove to wire racks to cool completely. Decorate with icing, if desired.

Makes about 2 dozen (5-inch) cookies

Chewy Chocolate Gingerbread Drops: Decrease flour to 1¾ cups. Shape 1½ teaspoonfuls of dough into balls. Place on ungreased cookie sheets. Flatten balls slightly. Do not refrigerate before baking. Bake as directed above. Makes about 4½ dozen cookies.

Chocolate Gingerbread Cookies

Chocolate Cherry Slices

⅓ cup red maraschino cherries, well drained
⅓ cup green maraschino cherries, well drained
 2 packages (about 16 ounces each) refrigerated sugar cookie
    dough
⅔ cup all-purpose flour, divided
   Red and green food colorings
 3 tablespoons unsweetened cocoa powder

1. Pat red cherries dry with paper towels. Finely chop; place in small bowl. Repeat with green cherries, placing in separate small bowl.

2. Remove dough from wrappers, keeping in log shapes. Cut each dough log into thirds, making six pieces total. Let dough stand at room temperature about 15 minutes.

3. Combine 2 pieces dough, ⅓ cup flour and red food coloring in medium bowl; beat with electric mixer at medium speed until well blended and evenly colored. Stir in red cherries. Repeat with 2 dough pieces, remaining ⅓ cup flour, green food coloring and green cherries. Wrap doughs separately in plastic wrap; refrigerate 15 minutes.

4. Combine remaining 2 dough pieces and cocoa in medium bowl; beat with electric mixer at medium speed until well blended. Wrap in plastic wrap; refrigerate 15 minutes.

5. Line 8×4-inch loaf pan with plastic wrap, extending wrap over sides. Pat red dough in even layer in prepared pan. Pat chocolate dough in even layer over red dough. Pat green dough in even layer over chocolate dough. Wrap tightly with plastic wrap. Freeze 2 hours.

6. Preheat oven to 350°F. Remove dough from pan; cut in half lengthwise. Cut each half into ¼-inch-thick slices. Place slices 2 inches apart on ungreased cookie sheets. Bake 10 to 12 minutes or until set. Cool on cookie sheets 1 minute; remove to wire racks to cool completely. *Makes about 5 dozen cookies*

Chocolate Cherry Slices

Christmas Tree Treats

1¾ cups all-purpose flour
½ teaspoon baking powder
¼ teaspoon salt
¾ cup plus 2 tablespoons (1¾ sticks) butter, softened
½ cup sugar
½ teaspoon almond extract
  Green food coloring
18 flat wooden popsicle sticks (at least 5 inches long)
  Prepared icings and decors (optional)

1. Combine flour, baking powder and salt in small bowl. Beat butter and sugar in large bowl with electric mixer at medium speed until well blended. Add almond extract; beat until well blended. Gradually add flour mixture, beating after each addition. Tint dough with food coloring until desired shade of green is reached. Divide dough in half; shape each half into 1-inch log. Wrap in plastic wrap; refrigerate 2 hours or until firm.

2. Preheat oven to 275°F. Lightly grease cookie sheets or line with parchment paper. Place wooden sticks on prepared cookie sheets. Cut dough into ¼-inch-thick slices. For each tree, place 3 slices next to each other half way up from bottom of stick; place 2 slices above them, overlapping bottom slices slightly. Place 1 slice at top of tree, overlapping middle slices slightly.

3. Bake 30 minutes or until edges are lightly browned. Cool on cookie sheets 5 minutes; remove to wire racks to cool completely. Decorate with icings and decors, if desired.   *Makes 1½ dozen large cookies*

Christmas Tree Treats

Rocky Road Crispy Treats

6 tablespoons butter
2 packages (10 ounces each) large marshmallows
1 package (12 ounces) semisweet chocolate chips, divided
12 cups crisp rice cereal (one 13½-ounce box)
1 (6-ounce) package sliced almonds (1⅔ cups), divided
2 cups mini marshmallows

1. Spray 13×9-inch baking pan with nonstick cooking spray.

2. Melt butter in large saucepan over low heat. Add large marshmallows; stir until completely melted. Stir in 1 cup chocolate chips until melted. Remove pan from heat; stir in cereal until well coated. Add remaining 1 cup chocolate chips, 1 cup almonds and mini marshmallows; stir to distribute evenly.

3. Press mixture into prepared pan with buttered hands, pressing down firmly to form even layer. Sprinkle with remaining ⅔ cup almonds. Cool completely before cutting. Serve immediately or store in airtight container up to 1 day.

Makes 2½ to 3 dozen treats

Quick Tip

Marshmallows tend to dry out quickly, so store them in the freezer in tightly sealed food storage bag to extend their shelf life. (Place the original bag inside a second bag before freezing.)

Rocky Road Crispy Treats

Melt-in-Your-Mouth
Christmas Marbles

½ cup (1 stick) butter, softened
6 tablespoons powdered sugar
¼ teaspoon vanilla
1 cup minus 2 tablespoons all-purpose flour
¼ teaspoon salt
    Red and green food coloring

1. Preheat oven to 350°F. Lightly grease cookie sheets or line with parchment paper.

2. Beat butter and powdered sugar in large bowl with electric mixer at medium speed until light and fluffy. Beat in vanilla until well blended. Gradually add flour and salt, beating after each addition.

3. Transfer half of dough to medium bowl; add red food coloring, beating until well blended and desired shade of red is reached. Add green food coloring to remaining half of dough, beating until well blended and desired shade of green is reached. For each marble, shape ½ teaspoonful of each color dough into one ball; place 1 inch apart on prepared cookie sheets.

4. Bake 12 to 14 minutes or until cookies are set. Cool on cookie sheets 2 minutes; remove to wire racks to cool completely.

Makes about 4 dozen cookies

Tip: To get the brightest colors, tint the dough with paste food coloring. Add a small amount of the paste coloring with a toothpick, then stir well. Slowly add more color until the dough is the desired shade. Paste food coloring is sold at specialty stores and comes in a wide variety of colors.

Melt-in-Your-Mouth Christmas Marbles

Yuletide Treasures

No-Bake Crunchy Chocolate Treasures

  1 package (5 ounces) waffle cones (12 cones)
  ¾ cup toffee bits
  ½ cup nut topping
  1 cup semisweet or bittersweet chocolate chips
  ⅓ cup chocolate hazelnut spread
     Holiday sprinkles and decors (optional)

1. Place waffle cones in large resealable food storage bag; seal bag. Crush cones into bite-size pieces with rolling pin. Combine crushed cones, toffee bits and nut topping in medium bowl.

2. Place chocolate chips in small microwavable bowl. Microwave on HIGH 1 minute or until chocolate is melted, stirring after 30 seconds. Immediately stir in chocolate hazelnut spread. Quickly fold chocolate mixture into toffee mixture; stir until well blended.

3. Place 42 foil-lined mini baking cups on baking sheet. Scoop 1 tablespoon chocolate mixture into each cup. Top with sprinkles, if desired. Refrigerate at least 2 hours before serving. Store in airtight container. *Makes about 3½ dozen treats*

No-Bake Crunchy Chocolate Treasures

Holiday Meringue Trees

 1 **cup pistachio nuts**
 4 **egg whites, at room temperature**
 ⅛ **teaspoon salt**
 ¾ **cup sugar**
 ½ **teaspoon vanilla**
   Green food coloring
20 **cinnamon-flavored graham cracker sticks**

1. Preheat oven to 250°F. Line cookie sheets with parchment paper. Place pistachios on clean dish towel; rub to remove excess skin. Finely chop pistachios.

2. Beat egg whites and salt in large bowl until foamy. Add sugar, ¼ cup at a time, beating until soft peaks form. Add vanilla; beat until stiff and glossy. Tint with food coloring until desired shade of green is reached. Fold in chopped pistachios.

3. Spoon mixture into pastry bag fitted with large writing or star tip. Pipe onto prepared cookie sheets in curved lines to make 3-inch tree shapes, allowing 1½ inches between trees. Insert graham cracker stick into base of each tree for trunk.

4. Bake 40 minutes or until firm to the touch, turning cookie sheets halfway through baking time. Turn oven off; let stand in oven 1½ hours. *Do not open oven door.* Remove to wire racks to cool completely. Store in single layer in airtight container.   *Makes about 20 cookies*

Note: Meringues are best when served within 24 hours.

Holiday Meringue Trees

Chocolate Strawberry Stackers

2½ cups powdered sugar, divided
1 cup (2 sticks) plus 6 tablespoons unsalted butter, softened, divided
2 tablespoons packed light brown sugar
½ teaspoon salt, divided
2 cups all-purpose flour
½ cup semisweet chocolate chips, melted
⅓ cup strawberry jam
½ teaspoon vanilla
1 to 2 tablespoons milk (optional)

1. Beat ½ cup powdered sugar, 1 cup butter, brown sugar and ¼ teaspoon salt in large bowl with electric mixer at medium speed 2 minutes or until light and fluffy. Gradually add flour, beating well after each addition. Beat in melted chocolate until well blended. Shape dough into 14-inch log. Wrap with plastic wrap; refrigerate 1 hour.

2. Preheat oven to 300°F. Cut log into ⅓-inch-thick slices; place on ungreased cookie sheets. Bake 15 to 18 minutes or until cookies are set and lightly browned. Cool on cookie sheets 5 minutes; remove to wire racks to cool completely.

3. Beat remaining 6 tablespoons butter in large bowl with electric mixer at medium speed until smooth. Beat in jam, vanilla and remaining ¼ teaspoon salt until blended. Gradually add remaining 2 cups powdered sugar; beat until fluffy. If mixture is too thick, gradually beat in milk until desired spreading consistency is reached. Spread frosting over flat sides of half of cookies; top with remaining cookies.   *Makes 21 sandwich cookies*

Variation: Substitute raspberry or apricot jam to create a more European flavor, or try pineapple or strawberry-rhubarb jam for a slightly more tart taste. Or, experiment with cherry, blueberry, blackberry or boysenberry jam to create a new family favorite.

Chocolate Strawberry Stackers

Cranberry Orange Crescents

2¼ cups all-purpose flour
¼ teaspoon salt
¼ teaspoon baking powder
1 cup (2 sticks) butter, softened
1 cup powdered sugar, divided
    Grated peel of 1 large orange
3 tablespoons orange juice
1 cup chopped sweetened dried cranberries
1 cup pecan halves, toasted* and finely chopped

*To toast pecans, spread in single layer on cookie sheet. Bake in preheated 350°F oven 8 to 10 minutes or until golden brown, stirring frequently.

1. Lightly grease cookie sheets or line with parchment paper.

2. Combine flour, salt and baking powder in small bowl. Beat butter, ¾ cup powdered sugar, orange peel and juice in large bowl with electric mixer at medium speed until well blended. Gradually add flour mixture, beating after each addition. Stir in cranberries and pecans.

3. Shape dough by rounded teaspoonfuls into 2-inch crescents; place 1 inch apart on prepared cookie sheets. Refrigerate 30 minutes.

4. Preheat oven to 350°F. Bake crescents 12 to 14 minutes or until edges are lightly browned. Remove to wire racks to cool slightly. Sprinkle remaining ¼ cup powdered sugar over warm cookies.

Makes about 6 dozen cookies

Cranberry Orange Crescents

Spiced Raisin Cookies with White Chocolate Drizzle

2 cups all-purpose flour
1½ teaspoons ground cinnamon
1 teaspoon baking soda
1 teaspoon ground ginger
½ teaspoon ground allspice
¼ teaspoon salt
1 cup sugar
¾ cup butter, softened
¼ cup molasses
1 egg
1 cup SUN-MAID® Raisins or Golden Raisins
4 ounces white chocolate, coarsely chopped

HEAT oven to 375°F.

COMBINE flour, cinnamon, baking soda, ginger, allspice and salt in small bowl. Set aside.

BEAT sugar and butter in large bowl until light and fluffy.

ADD molasses and egg; beat well.

BEAT in raisins. Gradually beat in flour mixture on low speed just until incorporated.

DROP dough by tablespoonfuls onto ungreased cookie sheets 2 inches apart. Flatten dough slightly.

BAKE 12 to 14 minutes or until set. Cool on cookie sheets 1 minute; transfer to wire racks and cool completely.

MICROWAVE chocolate in heavy, resealable plastic bag at high power 30 seconds. Turn bag over; heat additional 30 to 45 seconds or until almost melted. Knead bag with hands to melt remaining chocolate. Cut ⅛-inch corner off one end of bag. Drizzle cooled cookies with chocolate. Let stand until chocolate is set, about 20 minutes.

Makes about 2 dozen cookies

Prep Time: 15 minutes
Bake Time: 14 minutes

Spiced Raisin Cookies with White Chocolate Drizzle

Ginger Spice Thumbprints

2¼ cups all-purpose flour
1¾ teaspoons ground ginger
1½ teaspoons ground cinnamon
  1 teaspoon baking soda
  ¼ teaspoon salt
  ¾ cup packed light brown sugar
  ½ cup (1 stick) butter, softened
  ¼ cup molasses
  1 egg
    Granulated sugar
  ½ cup apricot, fig, plum or any flavor preserves

1. Preheat oven to 350°F. Lightly grease cookie sheets or line with parchment paper.

2. Combine flour, ginger, cinnamon, baking soda and salt in medium bowl. Beat brown sugar and butter in large bowl with electric mixer at medium speed until well blended. Add molasses and egg; beat until well blended. Gradually add flour mixture, beating after each addition.

3. Place granulated sugar in shallow bowl. Shape dough into 1-inch balls; roll in sugar to coat. Place 1½ inches apart on prepared cookie sheets. Press center of each ball with thumb; fill each indentation with ½ teaspoon preserves.

4. Bake 13 minutes or until edges are lightly browned. Cool on cookie sheets 1 minute; remove to wire racks to cool completely.

Makes about 4 dozen cookies

Ginger Spice Thumbprints

Pistachio Cookies

1 cup (2 sticks) butter, softened
¾ cup granulated sugar
¼ cup packed brown sugar
¼ cup unsweetened cocoa powder (optional)
1 teaspoon baking powder
¼ teaspoon ground nutmeg
1 egg
1½ teaspoons vanilla
2 cups all-purpose flour
1 cup coarsely chopped pistachio nuts

1. Beat butter, granulated sugar, brown sugar, cocoa, if desired, baking powder and nutmeg in large bowl with electric mixer at medium speed until creamy. Add egg and vanilla; beat until light and fluffy.

2. Stir in flour just until moist. Fold in pistachios. *Do not overmix.* Cover bowl with plastic wrap or damp cloth; refrigerate 1 hour.

3. Preheat oven to 350°F. Line cookie sheets with parchment paper. Shape dough by tablespoonfuls into balls; place 4 inches apart on prepared cookie sheets.

4. Bake 10 to 12 minutes or until set. Remove to wire racks to cool completely.   *Makes about 2 dozen cookies*

Pistachio Cookies

Chocolate Cherry Treats

½ cup (1 stick) butter, softened
¾ cup firmly packed light brown sugar
¼ cup granulated sugar
½ cup sour cream
1 large egg
1 tablespoon maraschino cherry juice
1 teaspoon vanilla extract
2 cups all-purpose flour
½ teaspoon baking soda
¼ teaspoon salt
1¼ cups "M&M's"® Milk Chocolate Mini Baking Bits
½ cup chopped walnuts
⅓ cup well-drained chopped maraschino cherries

Preheat oven to 350°F. In large bowl cream butter and sugars until light and fluffy; beat in sour cream, egg, maraschino cherry juice and vanilla. In medium bowl combine flour, baking soda and salt; add to creamed mixture. Stir in "M&M's"® Milk Chocolate Mini Baking Bits, walnuts and maraschino cherries. Drop by heaping tablespoonfuls about 2 inches apart onto ungreased cookie sheets. Bake about 15 minutes. Cool 1 minute on cookie sheets; cool completely on wire racks. Store in tightly covered container. *Makes 3 dozen cookies*

Chocolate Cherry Treats

Santa's Chocolate Cookies

1 cup (2 sticks) butter, cubed
⅔ cup semisweet chocolate chips
¾ cup sugar
1 egg
½ teaspoon vanilla
2 cups all-purpose flour
Melted semisweet chocolate, toasted coconut and sliced almonds (optional)

1. Combine butter and chocolate chips in large microwavable bowl. Microwave on HIGH 30 seconds; stir. Repeat as necessary until chips are melted and mixture is smooth. Let cool slightly. Add sugar, egg and vanilla; stir until well blended. Add flour; stir until well blended. Cover; refrigerate 30 minutes or until firm.

2. Preheat oven to 350°F. Shape dough by tablespoonfuls into balls; place 1 inch apart on ungreased cookie sheets. If desired, flatten balls with bottom of drinking glass.

3. Bake 8 to 10 minutes or until set. Remove to wire racks to cool completely. If desired, spread cookies with melted chocolate. Top with toasted coconut and sliced almonds, pressing to adhere.

Makes about 3 dozen cookies

 Quick Tip

To toast coconut for a cookie topping, spread evenly on an ungreased cookie sheet. Toast in a preheated 350°F oven for 5 to 7 minutes, stirring occasionally, until light golden brown.

Santa's Chocolate Cookies

Carrot Cake Cookies

1½ cups all-purpose flour
1 teaspoon ground cinnamon
½ teaspoon baking soda
½ teaspoon salt
¾ cup packed brown sugar
½ cup (1 stick) butter, softened
1 egg
½ teaspoon vanilla
1 cup grated carrots (about 2 medium)
½ cup chopped walnuts
½ cup raisins or chopped dried pineapple (optional)

1. Preheat oven to 350°F. Grease cookie sheets or line with parchment paper.

2. Combine flour, cinnamon, baking soda and salt in medium bowl. Beat brown sugar and butter in large bowl with electric mixer at medium speed until creamy. Add egg and vanilla; beat until well blended. Beat in flour mixture until blended. Stir in carrots, walnuts and raisins, if desired. Drop dough by rounded tablespoonfuls 2 inches apart onto prepared cookie sheets.

3. Bake 12 to 14 minutes or until set and edges are lightly browned. Cool on cookie sheets 1 minute; remove to wire racks to cool completely. *Makes about 3 dozen cookies*

Carrot Cake Cookies

Holiday
Express

Caramel-Kissed Pecan Cookies

  1 package (about 16 ounces) refrigerated sugar cookie dough
  ½ cup all-purpose flour
  1 package (2 ounces) ground pecans
 12 caramel-filled milk chocolate candy kisses, unwrapped
  1 package (2 ounces) pecan chips
    Caramel ice cream topping (optional)

1. Preheat oven 350°F. Line cookie sheet with parchment paper. Let dough stand at room temperature 15 minutes.

2. Beat dough, flour and ground pecans in medium bowl until well blended. Divide into 12 equal pieces. Place one candy in center of each piece of dough. Shape dough into ball around candies; seal well. Roll each ball in pecan chips. Place 2 inches apart on prepared cookie sheet.

3. Bake 16 to 18 minutes or until light golden brown around edges. Cool on cookie sheet 2 minutes.

4. If desired, warm caramel topping according to package directions; drizzle over warm cookies. Remove cookies to wire rack to cool completely. Store in airtight container.   *Makes 1 dozen cookies*

Caramel-Kissed Pecan Cookies

Snowball Bites

1 package (about 16 ounces) refrigerated sugar cookie dough
¾ cup all-purpose flour
2 tablespoons honey or maple syrup
1 cup chopped walnuts or pecans
   Powdered sugar

1. Let dough stand at room temperature 15 minutes.

2. Beat dough, flour and honey in large bowl with electric mixer at medium speed until well blended. Stir in walnuts. Shape dough into disc; wrap tightly in plastic wrap. Refrigerate at least 2 hours or up to 2 days.

3. Preheat oven to 350°F. Shape dough into ¾-inch balls; place 1½ inches apart on ungreased cookie sheets.

4. Bake 10 to 12 minutes or until lightly browned. Roll warm cookies in powdered sugar. Remove to wire racks to cool completely. Just before serving, roll cookies in additional powdered sugar.

Makes about 2½ dozen cookies

 Quick Tip

When working with sticky doughs, it helps to flour
or dampen your hands slightly with water; this
will prevent the dough from sticking.

Snowball Bites

Chocolate Cherry Gems

1 package (about 16 ounces) refrigerated sugar cookie dough
⅓ cup unsweetened Dutch process cocoa powder*
3 tablespoons maraschino cherry juice, divided
18 maraschino cherries, cut into halves
¾ cup powdered sugar

Dutch process cocoa gives these cookies an intense chocolate flavor and a dark, rich color. Other unsweetened cocoa powders can be substituted, but the flavor may be milder and the color may be lighter.

1. Preheat oven to 350°F. Lightly grease cookie sheets. Let dough stand at room temperature about 15 minutes.

2. Beat dough, cocoa and 1 tablespoon cherry juice in large bowl until well blended. Shape dough into ¾-inch balls; place 2 inches apart on prepared cookie sheets. Flatten balls slightly; press cherry half into center of each ball.

3. Bake 9 to 11 minutes or until set. Cool on cookie sheets 2 minutes; remove to wire racks to cool completely.

4. Combine powdered sugar and remaining 2 tablespoons cherry juice in small bowl; whisk until smooth. Add additional juice, 1 teaspoon at a time, if necessary, for medium-thick pourable glaze. Drizzle glaze over cooled cookies. Let stand until set. *Makes 3 dozen cookies*

Chocolate Cherry Gems

Christmas Wreaths

1 package (about 16 ounces) refrigerated sugar cookie dough
2 tablespoons all-purpose flour
Green food coloring
Green decorating sugar or sprinkles
Red decorating icing

1. Let dough stand at room temperature about 15 minutes.

2. Beat dough, flour and green food coloring in large bowl with electric mixer at medium speed until well blended and evenly colored. Divide dough in half; form each half into disc. Wrap both discs tightly with plastic wrap and freeze 20 minutes.

3. Preheat oven to 350°F. Grease cookie sheets. For cookie bottoms, roll 1 disc dough on lightly floured surface to ³⁄₈-inch thickness. Cut out dough with 3-inch round or fluted cookie cutter; place 2 inches apart on prepared cookie sheets. Using 1-inch round cookie cutter, cut out center from each cookie.

4. For cookie tops, roll remaining disc dough on lightly floured surface to ³⁄₈-inch thickness. Cut out dough with 3-inch round or fluted cookie cutter; place 2 inches apart on prepared cookie sheets. Using 1-inch round cookie cutter, cut out center from each cookie. Using hors d'oeuvre cutters, miniature cookie cutters or knife, cut out tiny shapes as shown in photo. Decorate with green sugar or sprinkles as desired.

5. Bake cookies 10 minutes or until very lightly browned at edges. Cool on cookie sheets 5 minutes; remove to wire racks to cool completely.

6. To assemble, spread icing on flat sides of cookie bottoms; place cookie tops over icing.   *Makes about 1½ dozen sandwich cookies*

Christmas Wreaths

Chocolate Toffee Crescents

1 package (about 16 ounces) refrigerated triple chocolate
    cookie dough
½ cup all-purpose flour
1 package (8 ounces) toffee baking bits, divided
¾ cup butterscotch chips or semisweet chocolate chips

1. Lightly grease cookie sheets. Let dough stand at room temperature about 15 minutes.

2. Beat dough and flour in large bowl with electric mixer at medium speed until well blended. Stir in 6 ounces toffee bits. Shape dough by rounded tablespoonfuls into crescent shapes; place 2 inches apart on prepared cookie sheets. Freeze 20 minutes.

3. Preheat oven to 350°F. Bake crescents 9 to 11 minutes or until set. Cool on cookie sheets 2 minutes; remove to wire racks to cool completely.

4. Place butterscotch chips in small resealable food storage bag. Microwave on MEDIUM (50%) 1 minute; knead bag lightly. Microwave and knead at additional 30-second intervals until completely melted. Cut off tiny corner of bag. Drizzle melted chips over crescents; sprinkle with remaining 2 ounces toffee bits. Let stand until set.

Makes about 2 dozen cookies

Chocolate Toffee Crescents

Peanut Butter Pixies

1 package (about 16 ounces) refrigerated peanut butter
    cookie dough
¼ cup all-purpose flour
1½ teaspoons ground cinnamon
¾ teaspoon ground ginger
½ teaspoon ground nutmeg
    Granulated sugar

1. Preheat oven to 350°F. Lightly grease cookie sheets. Let dough stand at room temperature 15 minutes.

2. Beat dough, flour, cinnamon, ginger and nutmeg in large bowl with electric mixer at medium speed until blended. Shape dough into ¾-inch balls; roll in sugar. Place 1 inch apart on prepared cookie sheets.

3. Bake 7 to 9 minutes or until edges are browned. Cool on cookie sheets 2 minutes; remove to wire racks to cool completely.

Makes 5 dozen mini cookies

Chocolate Gingersnaps

¾ cup sugar
1 package (about 18 ounces) chocolate cake mix *without*
    pudding in the mix
1 tablespoon ground ginger
2 eggs
⅓ cup vegetable oil

1. Preheat oven to 350°F. Spray cookie sheets with nonstick cooking spray. Place sugar in shallow bowl.

2. Combine cake mix and ginger in large bowl. Add eggs and oil; stir until well blended. Shape tablespoonfuls of dough into 1-inch balls; roll in sugar to coat. Place 2 inches apart on prepared cookie sheets.

3. Bake about 10 minutes. Remove cookies to wire racks to cool completely.

Makes about 3 dozen cookies

Peanut Butter Pixies

Spicy Oatmeal Combos

1 package (about 16 ounces) refrigerated sugar cookie dough
1 package (about 16 ounces) refrigerated oatmeal raisin cookie
      dough
¼ cup unsweetened cocoa powder
1¼ teaspoons ground ginger

1. Preheat oven to 350°F. Lightly grease cookie sheets. Let both packages of dough stand at room temperature 15 minutes.

2. Beat sugar cookie dough, cocoa and ginger in large bowl until well blended. Gently stir in oatmeal dough just until marbled. (Do not mix doughs thoroughly.) Shape dough into ¾-inch balls; place 2 inches apart on prepared cookie sheets.

3. Bake 8 to 10 minutes or until edges are lightly browned. Cool on cookie sheets 2 minutes; remove to wire racks to cool completely.

Makes about 4 dozen cookies

Quick Fruit & Lemon Drops

½ cup sugar
1 package (about 18 ounces) lemon cake mix
⅓ cup water
¼ cup (½ stick) butter, softened
1 egg
1 tablespoon grated lemon peel
1 cup mixed dried fruit bits

1. Preheat oven to 350°F. Grease cookie sheets. Place sugar in shallow bowl.

2. Beat cake mix, water, butter, egg and lemon peel in large bowl with electric mixer at low speed until well blended. Beat in fruit bits just until blended. Shape dough by heaping tablespoonfuls into balls; roll in sugar to coat. Place 2 inches apart on prepared cookie sheets.

3. Bake 12 to 14 minutes or until set. Cool on cookie sheets 2 minutes; remove to wire racks to cool completely.

Makes about 2 dozen cookies

Spicy Oatmeal Combos

Acknowledgments

The publisher would like to thank the companies listed below for the use of their recipes in this publication.

EAGLE BRAND®

The Hershey Company

© Mars, Incorporated 2008

Nestlé USA

Sun•Maid® Growers of California

Walnut Marketing Board

Index

A

Apricot
Apricot-Pecan Tassies, 14
Fruitcake Bars, 38
Ginger Spice Thumbprints, 70

B

Brownies
"Mexican" Brownies, 34
Ornament Brownies, 28
Perfectly Peppermint Brownies, 24
Butterscotch Toffee Gingersnap
    Squares, 22

C

Candy-Studded Wreaths, 2
Caramel-Kissed Pecan Cookies, 80
Carrot Cake Cookies, 78
Cherry
Chocolate Cherry Gems, 84
Chocolate Cherry Slices, 52
Chocolate Cherry Treats, 74
Chewy Chocolate Gingerbread Drops, 50
Chewy Pecan-Gingersnap Triangles, 36
Chocolate
Butterscotch Toffee Gingersnap
    Squares, 22
Caramel-Kissed Pecan Cookies, 80
Chewy Chocolate Gingerbread
    Drops, 50
Chocolate Cherry Gems, 84
Chocolate Cherry Slices, 52
Chocolate Cherry Treats, 74
Chocolate Gingerbread Cookies, 50
Chocolate Gingersnaps, 90
Chocolate Oatmeal Chippers, 12
Chocolate Strawberry Stackers, 64
Chocolate Toffee Crescents, 88
Chocolate Walnut Meringues, 20
Extra-Chocolatey Brownie Cookies, 4
Fruitcake Bars, 38
Holiday Buttons, 42
Holiday Treasure Cookies, 20
Malted Milk Cookies, 44
"Mexican" Brownies, 34
No-Bake Crunchy Chocolate
    Treasures, 60
Ornament Brownies, 28
Perfectly Peppermint Brownies, 24
Rocky Road Crispy Treats, 56
Santa's Chocolate Cookies, 76

Santa's Cookie Pizza, 46
Snowball Surprises, 6
Christmas Tree Treats, 54
Christmas Wreaths, 86
Coconut
Cranberry Coconut Bars, 32
Holiday Treasure Cookies, 20
Cookies, Bar
Butterscotch Toffee Gingersnap
    Squares, 22
Chewy Pecan-Gingersnap Triangles, 36
Cranberry Coconut Bars, 32
Cran-Orange Oatmeal Bars, 26
Fruitcake Bars, 38
Pumpkin Cheesecake Squares, 30
Santa's Cookie Pizza, 46
Cookies, Cutout
Chocolate Gingerbread Cookies, 50
Christmas Wreaths, 86
Cut-Out Cookies, 10
Gingerbread People, 8
Holiday Sugar Cookies, 16
Cookies, Drop
Carrot Cake Cookies, 78
Chocolate Cherry Treats, 74
Chocolate Oatmeal Chippers, 12
Chocolate Walnut Meringues, 20
Extra-Chocolatey Brownie Cookies, 4
Holiday Treasure Cookies, 20
Malted Milk Cookies, 44
Spiced Raisin Cookies with White
    Chocolate Drizzle, 68
Cookies, No-Bake
Crunchy Christmas Wreaths, 40
No-Bake Crunchy Chocolate
    Treasures, 60
Rocky Road Crispy Treats, 56
Cookies, Refrigerator
Chocolate Cherry Slices, 52
Chocolate Strawberry Stackers, 64
Christmas Tree Treats, 54
Holiday Buttons, 42
Cookies, Shaped
Apricot-Pecan Tassies, 14
Candy-Studded Wreaths, 2
Caramel-Kissed Pecan Cookies, 80
Chewy Chocolate Gingerbread Drops,
    50
Chocolate Cherry Gems, 84
Chocolate Gingersnaps, 90

Cookies, Shaped (*continued*)
Chocolate Toffee Crescents, 88
Cranberry Orange Crescents, 66
Ginger Spice Thumbprints, 70
Melt-in-Your-Mouth Christmas
    Marbles, 58
PB & J Thumbprint Cookies, 48
Peanut Butter Pixies, 90
Pistachio Cookies, 72
Pistachio Cranberry Biscotti, 18
Quick Fruit & Lemon Drops, 92
Santa's Chocolate Cookies, 76
Snowball Bites, 82
Snowball Surprises, 6
Spicy Oatmeal Combos, 92
Cranberries
Cranberry Coconut Bars, 32
Cranberry Orange Crescents, 66
Cran-Orange Oatmeal Bars, 26
Pistachio Cranberry Biscotti, 18
Cranberry Coconut Bars, 32
Cranberry Orange Crescents, 66
Cran-Orange Oatmeal Bars, 26
Crunchy Christmas Wreaths, 40
Cut-Out Cookies, 10

E
Extra-Chocolatey Brownie Cookies, 4

F
Fruitcake Bars, 38

G
Gingerbread People, 8
Ginger Spice Thumbprints, 70

H
Holiday Buttons, 42
Holiday Meringue Trees, 62
Holiday Sugar Cookies, 16
Holiday Treasure Cookies, 20

M
Malted Milk Cookies, 44
Melt-in-Your-Mouth Christmas Marbles,
    58
"Mexican" Brownies, 34

N
No-Bake Crunchy Chocolate Treasures,
    60

O
Oats
Chocolate Oatmeal Chippers, 12
Cranberry Coconut Bars, 32
PB & J Thumbprint Cookies, 48
Ornament Brownies, 28

P
PB & J Thumbprint Cookies, 48
Peanut Butter Pixies, 90
Peanuts
Butterscotch Toffee Gingersnap
    Squares, 22
PB & J Thumbprint Cookies, 48
Santa's Cookie Pizza, 46
Pecans
Apricot-Pecan Tassies, 14
Butterscotch Toffee Gingersnap
    Squares, 22
Caramel-Kissed Pecan Cookies, 80
Chewy Pecan-Gingersnap Triangles, 36
Cranberry Coconut Bars, 32
Cranberry Orange Crescents, 66
Fruitcake Bars, 38
Snowball Surprises, 6
Perfectly Peppermint Brownies, 24
Pistachios
Holiday Meringue Trees, 62
Pistachio Cookies, 72
Pistachio Cranberry Biscotti, 18
Powdered Sugar Glaze, 10
Pumpkin Cheesecake Squares, 30

Q
Quick Fruit & Lemon Drops, 92

R
Rocky Road Crispy Treats, 56

S
Santa's Chocolate Cookies, 76
Santa's Cookie Pizza, 46
Snowball Bites, 82
Snowball Surprises, 6
Spiced Raisin Cookies with White
    Chocolate Drizzle, 68
Spicy Oatmeal Combos, 92

W
Walnuts
Carrot Cake Cookies, 78
Chocolate Cherry Treats, 74
Chocolate Walnut Meringues, 20
Extra-Chocolatey Brownie Cookies,
    4
Snowball Bites, 82
White Chocolate
Fruitcake Bars, 38
Pistachio Cranberry Biscotti, 18
Santa's Cookie Pizza, 46
Spiced Raisin Cookies with White
    Chocolate Drizzle, 68